You Did It!

ISBN 978-0-6151-5526-5

Printed in the U.S.A.

Table of contents

Chapter One:
Why celebrating is so important

You've done a lot of fantastic things in your life.
You're going to do a lot more.
Now that's worth celebrating.

Don't dwell in the past!

We've often heard this expression throughout the course of our lives. The past is past; the future is now, don't look back, and so forth. We've been trained to let go, to move forward and to forget.

Consequently, a lot of us spend most of our time thinking about what's coming next - what do I have to do at work tomorrow, what am I going to make for dinner, how am I going to relax this weekend? We worry so much about what's next that we don't take the time to reflect on what has happened.

Late one night, I was lying in bed thinking about what I had to do the next day, when I realized that I was creating additional tension for myself at a time that should have been the most relaxing of the day.

So I cleared my head and tried to genuinely relax. It was then that a fond memory happened to jump into my head, bringing a smile to my face. I started thinking about a particular experience that brought me great joy when it happened several years ago, and I was soon feeling relaxed and content. The transition was instantaneous.

By calling upon a positive moment in my life, I was immediately relaxed, rejuvenated and ready for what comes next.

The next day I started to reflect on this change in mindset, and only then realized the powerful and positive influence it had on me both physically and emotionally.

In an effort to take this positive experience even further, I sat down and started to record all the positive things that have happened to me in my life. Things I'm proud of, experiences that bring a smile to my face, people who have made a positive impact on my life. After about twenty minutes, I had created quite a list of life experiences, all of which made me feel great.

All of us have done things that make us feel proud; things that make us laugh; things that put so much meaning into our lives. These memories and accomplishments are our most prized possession. It's about time we celebrated those moments.

So let's give it a try. In the spaces provided below, write five of the best moments in your life. Don't think about it too hard; simply write the first five that come to mind. Go!

Five of the best moments in your life.

_____

_____

_____

_____

_____

See? That wasn't so hard. Now pick one of the five items listed above and take a few moments to stop and really think back to that time.

Go ahead, close your eyes and take yourself there.

If you took the time to stop and think about one of the items on the previous page, chances are you've got a smile on your face right now.

Whether you're eighteen or seventy-eight, you've done some amazing things in your life. In fact there are probably hundreds of times you've experienced truly happy moments. These memories are the foundation that gives you strength, contentment and an inherent excitement to find out what comes next. Your past isn't something to tuck away into the deep recesses of your mind; it's something to celebrate and reflect upon to help you with the next adventure heading your way.

This book can help you celebrate some of the best moments in your life and use those positive feelings and experiences to carry you forward.

So when you're lying in bed tonight, and a million things are running through your head, pick one of the items on this list and clear everything else from your mind. Think back to this outstanding moment and smile. No sleeping pill can do a better job of relaxing you for a great night's rest.

Great moments shouldn't be kept in the back of your mind. They should be celebrated as a source of inspiration, pride and strength.

Every day of your life, you're creating memories. Most adults can remember moments as far back as age three. That means the typical 30-year-old adult has about 9,855 days worth of potential memories. If you consider how many memorable events happen each day, that number starts multiplying exponentially. However, the brain isn't programmed to keep that much information in its long-term banks. That's why out of a given week, only a handful of events will permanently be stored. Only those moments that truly have an impact on us physically, emotionally and psychologically will be moved to long-term memory. The ones that remain are there for a reason. These are the moments, good and bad, that have molded and transformed your life. But just because they've already happened doesn't mean you can't continue to use these moments to affect you in new ways.

By thinking back to a time in our lives when we experienced happiness, accomplishment, satisfaction, etc., the brain allows us to relive those emotions, thereby creating an instantaneous effect. By recalling those fond memories and events, we can easily lift ourselves up in the present.

Think about that for a minute... you have the ability to stir up these positive emotions anytime you wish. That's a very powerful tool at your disposal.

Some people might interpret this as "living in the past," and will claim that dwelling on past experiences can be detrimental if done to such an extreme as to interfere with one's continual development. But there's a difference between living in the past and using past experiences to help us progress in our daily lives. Reflecting on what has happened in your life can help you prepare for and celebrate what comes next.

Overcoming negative influences

Unfortunately, we encounter negative situations every day of our lives. We get stuck in traffic. The line at the post office is out the door. A co-worker is being a real jerk. The list goes on and on (and on).

You've heard the old adage, "The problem isn't important. What's important is how you deal with it." Nothing could be more true. We're all going to have new issues to deal with on a regular basis. But this has been true every day of your adult life. So, what's new? Every single day leading up this one, you've been dealing with situations. Some of them have been relatively minor. Some have been life-changing. But in every case, you chose an option on how to deal with the situation. You've also learned more about what options have and haven't worked. This knowledge is helping you to continually grow as an individual; and you'll continue to learn every day as you face new situations.

This leads us to another powerful benefit of recalling past accomplishments and experiences – learning from ourselves.

You are the most influential, effective and engaging teacher you'll ever meet. Think about that for a minute. Sure, you may or may not be the best at teaching others; but over the years, you've taught yourself more than anyone else in the world could have. And you're not finished. You're teaching yourself new things every day.

So we've established how effective a teacher you are (at least to yourself)... now we need to work on your skills as a student. If you learn to listen a little better, you'll learn even more from yourself than you can imagine.

So let's begin. On the following pages, write the greatest accomplishments you've achieved in your life. These are specific events that make you feel a genuine sense of pride. It doesn't have to be monumental; just because you haven't climbed Everest doesn't mean you don't have plenty of things to be proud of. It could be something as simple as helping your brother pass his seventh-grade algebra class. But list any and all events that have filled you with a sense of accomplishment.

Here are some example ideas to help get you started:

- Getting promoted to manager while working at ABC company
- Helping that injured puppy by taking him to the vet
- Teaching yourself how to sail
- Getting an A on your term paper in 10th grade English
- Anything you want to list

When creating your list, try to be as specific as possible. Think back to that moment and write down exactly what happened.

This one will require some thought, so take several minutes to really think back through your life. And don't skimp on yourself - if you did it and it made you feel good, write it down. Think all the way back to your childhood and create a mental timeline going forward to today. Write down everything you've accomplished.

(Don't worry if your list doesn't take up both pages. It's not the number of accomplishments in your life, it's the quality. And if you need more than two pages to capture everything you've done, there are plenty of blank notes pages in the back of this book.)

Go for it. Turn to pages 9-10 and begin your list.

Your greatest accomplishments

_____

_____

_____

_____

_____

_____

_____

_____

_____

_____

_____

_____

_____

_____

_____

_____

Your greatest accomplishments, continued

_____

_____

_____

_____

_____

_____

_____

_____

_____

_____

_____

_____

_____

Now take a moment to reflect on your big list of accomplishments.

Take a look at the list you just created. Nobody else in the entire world has done what you've accomplished. As amazing as that sounds, it's entirely true. Others may have similar accomplishments, but this list in its entirely is wholly unique to only you. These are moments where you positively impacted your life and the lives of others. Be proud of this list, because it's no small feat. Go ahead, take a few moments and reflect on all you've done.

Now take a break. Put this book down and finish your day. If you encounter any less-than-pleasant moments, stop and think about one of the items on your list. Conversely, if you encounter any outstanding moments, be sure to add that to your list. That's the most exciting element about this process... *your list will never be finished.*

Chapter Two:
Learning From Your Accomplishments

*Use your accomplishments
to map out your strengths,
your opportunities and your
potential for growth.*

Now it's time to put your big list to good use. All of the things you wrote down happened in the past. But that doesn't mean they can't help you going forward. To the contrary, these events and experiences are what have shaped you as an individual, and provide you with the necessary context and knowledge to help you do great things ahead. You've already made the crucial first step – capturing on paper your life's accomplishments. Now it's time to take it a step further and begin the process of analyzing these events to look for ways to further use them going forward.

We'll start with evaluating the accomplishments that have to do with your professional life. Go back to your list of accomplishments on pages 9-10 and take note of any that are related to work. (If you are a student or work at home, look for those related accomplishments.) Now re-write those particular moments in the space provided below.

Professional accomplishments

_____

_____

_____

_____

_____

_____

_____

For each of these targeted accomplishments, think through the following question:

What skills and/or knowledge did you use to help you with the accomplishment? (Use the spaces below to write down your answers.)

_____

_____

_____

_____

_____

_____

_____

The attributes you just listed are those that have helped you do great things in your career. These are your true strengths that allow you to excel. As your career continues to develop (or if you're exploring a new career), look for projects that would allow you to apply these skills for future successes. This isn't always easy, as oftentimes we don't have direct input on the projects we're presented with. But when the opportunity arises, you'll know it. (And will be better able to achieve success more quickly.)

Go ahead. Do some bragging.

These work-related accomplishments are something to celebrate, and can be used to help pave the way for future successes. Start a dialogue with your boss. Let him/her know all that you have achieved.

"Bragging" about oneself is something most people shy away from. They think it would be too boastful to talk about one's successes with their boss. But how else will your manager know all that you've done and all that you can do? Sure, he/she knows about some of the great things you've done. But it's highly unlikely that your manager can recite all of your notable accomplishments. If you do it right, it won't sound boastful at all; and your manager will appreciate you sharing the information.

Consider this… your boss has been tasked with developing a new project. Although she's incredibly busy, she wants the new project to be a sure success, so she oversees it personally. The following two scenarios are common in a case like this:

1. Because she's not entirely certain who on her team can handle important tasks related to the new project, she takes them on personally. After all, that way she knows they'll be done right.

2. She delegates important project tasks to those who she knows will do a great job. The team is therefore able to complete the project more quickly, with better results.

Obviously, the second scenario is the better of the two. But more often than not, managers in today's business world lean toward the first scenario, simply because they're not immediately aware of their associates' strengths.

You can fix this.

While most managers are too busy to stop and think about all the outstanding things their team members have contributed, you can remedy this by doing the work for your boss. Prepare a list to share with your manager, highlighting the particular skills and knowledge where you're most proficient. Not only will they appreciate you bringing this information to them, but will also be more likely to assign you important projects going forward. There's no better way to move ahead in the business world.

See what a little bragging can do?

I know… easier said than done. After all, how do you approach your manager to try and let him/her know how great you are?

Here's something that might help. On the following page is a sample dialogue to help you set up and prepare for a meeting with your boss to talk through your list of accomplishments. There's also room for you to adapt the information to fit your particular situation.

Note: the example on the following page works for those of us with a boss. However, if you happen to be the boss, you can adapt this process by proactively collecting lists of accomplishments from each of your team members. After all, the more you know about the strengths of each of your associates, the better you'll be able to delegate projects and tasks.

Preparing for the meeting

Hi (manager's name).

If you have time during the next day or two, I'd like to schedule a half-hour with you to talk through some ideas on how I can further contribute to future projects. I've made an inventory of my professional skills, experience and knowledge that may help you the next time you're looking for assistance with a particular task. What day/time would work best for you?

Thank you.

Use the space below to take this sample and rewrite it to best fit your situation.

During the meeting

Thank you for meeting with me. I know you have a lot on your plate, so I wanted to take just a few minutes to let you know that I'm willing to help with new projects. Here's a quick rundown of what I've accomplished professionally.

(Run through list of accomplishments.)

These are the skills and traits that I'm able to use well:

(Run through the list of skills and knowledge areas.)

If you have an upcoming project where this set of skills and experience would allow me contribute, please keep me in mind.

Again, use the space below to take this sample and rewrite it to best fit your situation.

The scenario just described accomplishes a couple of things. First of all, it shows initiative. And initiative can go a very long way in furthering your career. Secondly, it helps your manager by allowing him/her to better understand your strengths. The next time an important project comes up, who's the first person your manager will think of? You. So give it a try.

Sharing is a two-way street.

Now that you've shared some of your best moments with your boss/professor/spouse (or whomever), it's the perfect time to stop and ask that person about some of their greatest moments. Allowing him/her to contribute to the conversation accomplishes a couple of things:

- People like talking about themselves, and will appreciate that you asked.

- You'll be in a better position to understand what is important to that person, which will allow you to match up your skills and knowledge to his/her needs.

By understanding others' achievements, you'll benefit from knowing more about what makes them "tick," and be able to understand them better.

We've now seen how reflecting on our past accomplishments can help open doors to success going forward. But this is only one way in which our best moments can benefit us.

Let's switch gears now, and think through how we can use our past accomplishments to enhance our personal lives.

What makes us happy in life? What are the things that bring a smile to our faces and remind us why life is so important? Here are a few of the things a lot of people commonly list:

- Family
- Friends
- Success
- Memories
- Love
- Giving
- Hope
- Toys (material things)
- The arts
- Vacations

The items listed above are broad categories of some things that bring people happiness. But let's drill down to the specific items that bring you the most happiness in your life. On the following pages, list as many of the things, people, places and feelings that affect you most.

The things that bring you the most happiness

_____

_____

_____

_____

_____

_____

_____

_____

_____

_____

_____

_____

_____

_____

The things that bring you the most happiness, continued

_____

_____

_____

_____

_____

_____

_____

_____

_____

_____

_____

_____

_____

_____

The list you just created is extremely important, because these are the things that ground you – people, places, feelings and accomplishments that make you who you are. Obviously, this is just a partial list. But it will help you keep the important things in mind.

Take a few moments to think about the list you just completed. Then compare this with the list of greatest accomplishments you created on pages 9-10. How many of the items were common between both lists? The most important difference between the two is the fact that you have complete control over your list of accomplishments. These are things that you did. The list you just created on the previous pages contains items that may or may not be under your control. For example, while our families often bring us much joy, we don't have complete control over each member's actions. After all, they're individuals and are making independent decisions every day.

Both lists are equally important, however. Each can be used to help you focus on the positive things in your life that give you strength and relax you when you need it most. The following situations are when you'll need these lists the most:

- When you're stressed
- When you need to relax
- When you're looking for inspiration
- When you just want to feel good
-
-
-
-

What else? In the spaces above, write other situations where your lists can help you.

So what now? How do we use all this information to better our lives going forward? The answer is simple... keep it handy.

I'm not talking about keeping the lists physically close to you; keeping it handy means being able to mentally call upon some of your greatest memories, accomplishments and sources of happiness as you encounter tough situations.

Let's consider a specific example of how our personal achievements, combined with the list of things that bring us happiness, can help us in our personal lives.

One common situation a lot of us encounter is a tough day at work. We've all had them... we will all continue to have them. But you know what? It's time to stop worrying about it. *Traffic was horrendous coming into work?* So what. *Your boss didn't give you credit for doing a good job?* Big deal. This stuff happens every day.

Instead of letting these daily annoyances get to you, think about the great accomplishments you've done in your life and about those things and those people that bring an instant smile to your face.

Here's the really great part... the more you stop letting these things get to you, the less you'll notice them happening.

Time for a test...

You're on your lunch break, and you have a couple of errands to run. It's 105 degrees outside, and the air conditioning in your car has stopped working. You stop at a gas station to fill up, but the credit card reader at the pump is out of order, so you have to run inside to pay. There's only one person working there (and he doesn't look like he knows what he's doing), so the line is literally out the door. You're going to be there in line for at least ten minutes. Since you're not going anywhere for a few minutes, you have a couple of choices -- you can either stand there and think about all the things that aren't going your way today, or you can take a moment to think about something that brings an instant smile to your face. This can be something from your lists or it can be something great that happened to you the day before.

Don't dwell on the all the aggravating stuff that hits you. I know - you've heard this a thousand times before from all kinds of sources - but this time I want you to really think about what happens when you dwell on the negative.

Right now, I'd like you to do the following: look across the room and find a small, inanimate object at least five feet away from you (lamp, vase, etc.). Now I'd like you to think really hard about that object and move it toward you using only your mind.

C'mon. Hurry up.

What's the matter?

You can't do it, because it can't be done. (Perhaps in theory, but nobody has ever actually proved they could do it.) This is exactly the same as sitting there worrying about a problem or bad situation. Thinking about it isn't going to solve the problem. What it will do is cause you frustration and stress. So stop it!

In our lunch-time example above, thinking about everything that's gone wrong isn't going to get you to the cashier any faster. All it's going to do is make the situation worse (for you and those around you).

Let's consider another example. Suppose you were having a water cooler discussion with a co-worker and threw out some less-than-complimentary comments about your boss. But what you didn't realize was that your boss was standing right behind you during the conversation. She didn't say anything at the time, but you know she heard at least a portion of your comments.

For the rest of the day, and well into the night, you sat there and worried about how much she heard and how she now feels about you as a result. But did all that worrying do anything to solve the problem? No. All it did was make your evening miserable, and probably did the same for those who interacted with you.

In a situation like the one described above, you basically have three choices:

1. Worry about the situation until you get back to work the next day.
2. Clear it from your head, enjoy your evening, and deal with it when you see your boss again.
3. Call her immediately, apologize and see how mad she really is.

The first option does you no good whatsoever. In fact, it has been proven that excessive worrying can be detrimental to one's health. So don't do it. (I know... easier said than done.)

The second option is much better than the first; but unless you're a robot, it's extremely difficult to do. Human nature is to worry about what's going to happen next.

The third option, if feasible at the time, it the most preferable. Face the issue head on, as soon as you can. That way, you'll be able to stop worrying about the unknown and can begin working on a solution.

So what if option three isn't feasible at the time? What if you tried calling your boss, but she didn't answer the phone?

In this situation, there are things you can do to help forget about the problem until you are able to deal with it. For example, if you aren't able to contact your boss until the following day, sit down and make a plan for correcting the situation. Write down different ways you can apologize, depending on where you might encounter her. Think back to previous times in your life when you either delivered or received a successful apology. What made it so successful? Then try to incorporate some of those elements.

Once you've finished that process, you can relax, knowing that there's nothing more you can do until you see her the next day. Move on and focus on more positive things.

Again... not worrying about things we can't control is easy to talk about, but not-so-easy to put into practice. Here are some things that can help...

1. Every time you start to worry about something, ask yourself the following question:

Is there anything I can do right now that will help the situation?

If the answer is yes, then do that. If the answer is no, then pull up one of your positive moments and get your mind off the problem.

2. Talk about it. Sit down with or call someone you can trust (co-worker, family member or friend). Explain the problem that you're facing. Many times, just speaking with someone else about the issue will present new solutions that you hadn't previously considered.

Once you're finished speaking with your confidant, get the problem out of your head until you can actually do something about it.

3. Remember this acronym: **W.I.S.E.** (worrying is silly every time)

So be wise!

Chapter Three:
The Importance of Confidence

"When you have confidence, you can have a lot of fun.
And when you have fun, you can do amazing things. "
- Joe Namath

Self-confidence is a weird thing. It provides us the ability to do amazing things, yet we spend a lot of time and energy fighting off being confident.

Think about the last time you said this to yourself:

"There's no way I could do that..."

Even though confidence is a critically important part of our success, most of us are naturally reluctant to allow ourselves to be confident. We're constantly shooting ourselves down. The silly part of all this is, as soon as you say the above to yourself, it becomes true. If you don't think you can do something, you won't be able to. It sounds cliché, I know. But it's true.

There are a few reasons why a lot of us have a tendency to guard against building confidence.

1. We don't think we're good enough or smart enough

2. Fear of becoming boastful or cocky

3. We're afraid of failing, so we quit before we even try

4. We're just kind of lazy

Let's look at each one of these in turn…

We don't think we're good enough or smart enough

No matter the situation, there's always that little voice in the back of our minds that it sitting there saying, "Are you sure? I don't think you should do that." This voice can be a good thing. If you're contemplating a base jump off a skyscraper during high winds, it's probably a good idea to listen to this voice. But this voice can also be very detrimental to your success in life. In many cases, this voice starts spewing off, causing high levels of self-doubt, when there's no real basis for a lack of confidence. Here's an example of what I'm talking about (taken from personal experience)...

Many years ago, I had a great idea on how our department could improve the way we do things. Being relatively new to the company, I wasn't sure if I should share it with my boss or not. Although the company had an "open door" policy that encouraged the open sharing of ideas, this particular idea meant drastically changing certain practices. Here are some samples of the thoughts that ran through my head as I contemplated whether or not to submit this idea:

"Why would they listen to a 'newbie' who's only been here ten minutes?"
"You don't know enough about this place yet. Wait until you're more established before bringing this up."
"Are you nuts? Shut up, and don't rock the boat."

There are a hundred more negative thoughts I could list here, but you get the point. I was doing my absolute best to talk myself out of presenting this idea to management – even though deep down, I knew it was the right thing to do.

So what did I do? I told that little voice to cram it, and put a proposal together on how this one idea could significantly benefit the company. I created a presentation and an executive summary, and submitted it to my boss.

Three days later, a copy of the executive summary was sitting back on my desk, with two words written on it... "Won't work."

Needless to say, I was a little devastated. I had put all this time and effort into shaping the idea into a proposal, and my boss shot it right down. About this time, I was sitting there wondering why I hadn't listened to that little voice. But then an amazing thing happened... my boss suddenly left the company, and I was approached by the department VP. He had seen a copy of my proposal sitting on my former boss' desk, and took the time to read through it. He not only liked what I had written, but he gave me my boss' job.

It was right then that I swore off listening to that idiotic little voice. If I had succumbed to all that self-doubt, I would have missed an outstanding opportunity at one great promotion.

So unless I find myself standing on the edge of a building with a parachute on my back, that little voice is going to have a hard time getting through.

The next time self-doubt tries to talk you out of trying something that's out of your comfort zone, tell that little voice to go fly a kite. Something amazing just might happen.

In fact, let's take a couple of minutes to apply this to your personal situation. In the spaces below, write down five things that you've wanted to do, but didn't (or haven't) because of that damn little voice.

_____

_____

_____

_____

_____

I'm not recommending you always throw caution to the wind. But before you rule something out just because you think you're not the best person, try this... say to yourself, "I can definitely do this." Then decide if it's the best course of action. By simply stopping for a minute and giving yourself a little affirmation, you can help cancel out those feelings of inadequacy. And that will help you make the right decision on whether or not to proceed.

We don't want to be cocky

Whether it's playing tennis, creating a report, making your sales quota or impressing a date, confidence is what will allow you to do the best you can. It gives you that little edge that makes ordinary people do great things.

But another prevalent reason why we don't allow ourselves to be self-confident is that we guard against being overconfident. We've all been around that guy (or girl) who thought he knew way more than the rest of the group. We don't like him, and we certainly don't want to be like him. So we play it safe and downplay our abilities- even to ourselves.

The problem is, we can be pretty brutal critics when it comes to analyzing our own thoughts and actions. So we tend to limit ourselves more than we should, and get in our own way of success.

Think of it this way... if there's a boxing match between someone who is extremely confident and one who lacks self-confidence, who's going to be the odds-on favorite? Nine times out of ten, the latter fighter is going down in the first round.

Let's put this into a practical situation... when was the last time you were in a meeting, at a party, in the classroom, etc., where you had an interesting point to make, but didn't offer it because you thought it would be stating the obvious? Well, it may be obvious to you, but I guarantee you there are several people in the room who could benefit from hearing it. What's obvious to you may be just the idea the group was looking for (or at least steer the topic in the right direction).

This doesn't mean you should just spout out anything that pops into your head. But don't worry about what other might think about your idea. Even if you think it sounds "cocky," someone else in the room is going to be glad you brought it up. Remember, you are your own toughest critic. Don't over-censor yourself.

> *The most important part of being great at something is knowing that you're going to be great at it. Turn off that censor chip in your brain for a minute and really allow yourself to do something amazing.*

Remember -- you're in control of how much self-confidence you have. It's completely up to you how you view your abilities. So don't hold back. Give yourself the power to be great.

We're afraid of failing, so we quit before we try

This one ties somewhat into the previous section on not having self-confidence. But it goes even deeper than that. For many of us, not only do we limit ourselves on how much self-confidence we have, but we negate our abilities so much that we convince ourselves we won't succeed before we even consider trying something (no matter how unjustified those thoughts may be).

Here's an example to help explain the point. A friend of mine shared an experience where she was contemplating a job change because her existing situation was something less than desirable. But her job was pretty specialized, and she didn't (in her mind) have a lot of skills outside that scope. So every time she came across an ad for a job that sounded good, she would immediately discount herself because she didn't think she could do it. (This is actually a pretty common scenario.) But then something wonderful happened – she got fired. Because she now felt pressured to find a job quickly, she was forced into rethinking the types of jobs she could and couldn't do. That's when the shift occurred.

She started interviewing for positions the she otherwise would not have even considered. The more she learned about some of these other jobs, the more she realized that she could do them. She also began to recognize that it had less to do about particular skills; it was more about her attitude and her outlook.

It was amazing to me how you could see the change in her, both mentally and physically. Her demeanor changed. Her smile changed. Her self-confidence increased, and she started nailing interviews. It wasn't long before she found a fantastic job. (She now heads up a department at a very successful corporation, and is exponentially happier with her career.) And to think... had she not been fired from that dead-end job, she would still be working there, miserable, thinking she wouldn't be able to succeed in a different role.

This example just goes to show that sometimes we need to shut up for a minute and quit over-analyzing our decisions. Why do you think Nike's slogan has been around for so long? Because it sums it up quite nicely – Just Do It.

We're just kinda lazy

This one's my favorite. Not because it's any more interesting, but because it's the one I'm most guilty of (as are a lot of people). After all, trying something new and building up enough self-confidence to do it well takes a lot of work.

What compounds this issue is the fact that we're all pretty busy people. We've got jobs, hectic family life, school, shopping, and a thousand other things on our plates every day. How can we possibly find time to think through things like building self-confidence? Besides... when I finally do get some time to myself, I just want to relax. So I'll get to it later.

But you know what? Later never comes. That's why being busy is not a good excuse. We're always going to be busy. But every one of us can find more time if we really put our minds to it. Besides, "busy" is a relative concept.

Many years ago, I heard a comedian make a statement in his routine that really stuck with me. He stated, "We've gotten pretty lazy over the years. My dad worked three jobs after I was born to make ends meet. He would literally leave one job and go to the next. Nowadays, if I have to do the laundry, that's it – I'm done for the day."

Let's face it... for the most part, we have it easier than our parents and grandparents had it. Over the past couple of decades, life has gotten easier (for most of us). So don't give me that "I'm too busy" story. You can find time. You just have to do it. Don't get in the way of your own success by thinking you don't have time to get it right.

Building self-confidence takes work. Whether it's working on your presentation skills, getting in shape or even learning a new skill, you have to devote time to getting better and better at it. But with so many other things that need to get done in a day, how do we find time to do all of this?

This is one easy answer -- stop procrastinating. Don't put off what you know you need to do. I know, I know... easier said than done. But in many cases, procrastination develops out of confusion between what's important and what's urgent.

Let's say, for example, that you want to work on learning more about your company's technical products. So you tell yourself, "I'm going to spend at least 15 minutes a day reading through the technical manuals." But by the time you check e-mail, return phone calls, go to lunch with your co-workers and finish everything else you were supposed to do that day, there's just no time left to read those manuals. (And forget about trying to do it at home with three kids to care for...)

The thing is, if you were able to rewind your day and take a hard look at everything you did, chances are you would find plenty of opportunity to fit in that 15-minute study period. We typically spend a lot of time on things that are urgent, but not necessarily important. (Or even worse, things that are neither urgent nor important.)

So the next time you're at work, think through everything that you need to accomplish that day and place them into one of four categories:

1. Important and urgent
2. Important but not urgent
3. Urgent but not important
4. Neither urgent nor important

Use the following chart to help you. Once you've placed your to-do items in the appropriate quadrant, re-prioritize them from left to right, top to bottom. So an item that is important but not urgent will take precedence over an item that is urgent but not important.

You'll be amazed at how much extra time you'll find in the day by not devoting time to things that really aren't that important.

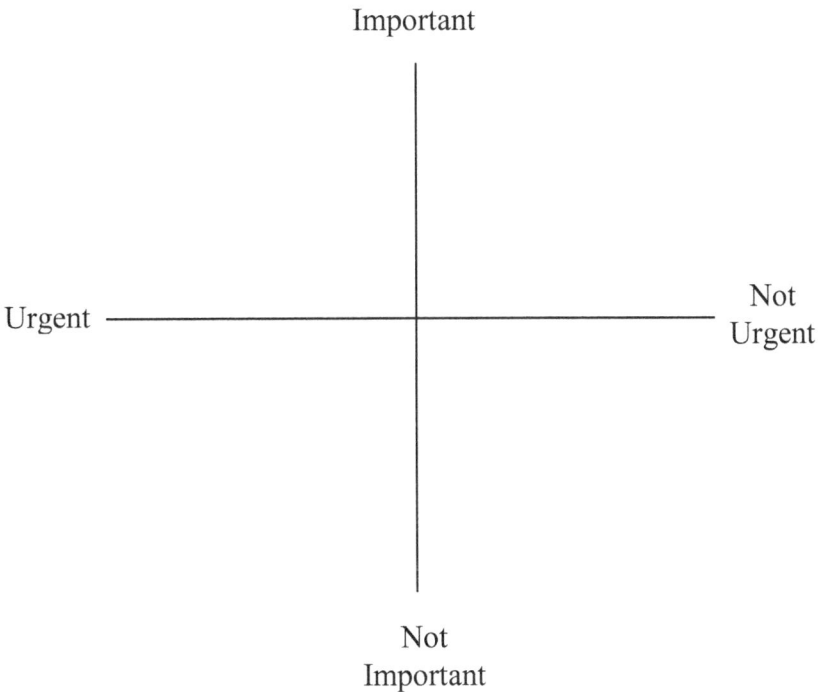

Important

Urgent ——————————————— Not
                                      Urgent

Not
Important

Chapter four:
The Big Seven

Cherish your time...
Ah, forget it.

1. Live life to the fullest.

Yeah, yeah. We've all heard it before. Sure, it's a very important point. But unfortunately, the point has become muddled through an endless variety of platitudes that have made the notion trite.

Any of these sound familiar?

- Life is short; make the best of it.
- We don't have a lot of time; cherish every moment.
- Don't take things for granted.

Again, these are all very important thoughts. But the meaning has been lost, and we just don't pay any real attention to them anymore. We simply nod our heads and say, "That's so true..." without realizing what it really means. I know, because I was just as guilty as the next person.

Then, while watching a movie one day, I heard it said a little differently. And it was just enough to make me stop and really think about what was being said.

> *"My father says that almost the whole world is asleep. Everybody you know. Everybody you see. Everybody you talk to. He says that only a few people are awake – and they live in a state of constant, total amazement."*
> - Joe Versus The Volcano

I suddenly realized that I was asleep, and had been for quite some time. I went through each and every day without realizing what was going on around me. I would have an occasional moment when I would open my eyes just long enough to notice something really great happening; but for the most part, I was asleep. A lot of things were passing by without me recognizing their brilliance.

So I decided to wake up.

And it was amazing. I started to see how even the smallest things are works of wonder: the view from my back yard, the smell of freshly peeled oranges, a goldfish swimming in an aquarium. Everything around you is amazing when you stop and really think about it.

This doesn't mean walking around in a stupor, saying how beautiful everything is. But it does mean allowing yourself to stop and appreciate the important things that impact our lives (and even those things that don't seem that important).

Here's the really tough part... waking yourself up. A lot of people will read all of this and say, "You're right... I'm going to appreciate things more." Yet nothing will really change for them. Here's something that may help.

On the next couple of pages, write down anything and everything that are amazing to you. Start with the obvious ones (family, friends, etc.), then start to think through those things that may be less obvious – the changing of the leaves, refrigerators, a song that really gets you dancing. Stretch yourself and really give it some thought.

Go ahead... I'll wait.

Things that are amazing to you

_____

_____

_____

_____

_____

_____

_____

_____

_____

_____

_____

_____

_____

_____

Things that are amazing to you, continued

_____

_____

_____

_____

_____

_____

_____

_____

_____

_____

_____

_____

If you run out of room, there are blank pages in the back.

Nice work. Now go back to the list you just created, and put an asterisk next to every item that you have been taking for granted. Be honest with yourself...

> *"When something does not insist on being noticed, when we aren't grabbed by the collar or struck on the skull by a presence or an event, we take for granted the very things that most deserve our gratitude."*
> *- Cynthia Ozick*

Okay – so we've identified some things that are pretty amazing when you stop and think about it, and we've acknowledged that we've been doing some sleepwalking of our own. That's an important first step toward waking up and really appreciating life.

Now pick one item on the list you just created. At some point before you go to bed tonight, take a moment and think about how that one thing makes your life better.

Then - tomorrow - pick another one.

2. Mix it up.

By mixing things up, we break patterns. By breaking patterns, we open our eyes to new and exciting things.

Change can be a good thing. It keeps us on our toes, and reinvigorates us (sometimes when we need it most). It doesn't have to be monumental change – it could be something as minor as cooking a meal you've never tried before. The point is, we get stuck in our daily routines which become pervasive in our lives, numbing us to what's going on outside these routines. By mixing things up, we break those patterns and start opening our eyes to new things.

In some cases, we need significant change in our lives (we're in a bad situation at work, etc.) but we're so paralyzed by the fear of change that we do nothing to better the situation. So start small. Get used to change by introducing it into your life everyday. Then, when it comes time for more significant change in your life, you'll be much more receptive to embracing that opportunity.

So where do we begin? Here's a list to help get you started. These are items that are easy to do, yet will help you become more comfortable with change. (Try coming up with your own in the spaces provided below.)

- Try a restaurant you've never been to
- Park on the other side of the garage
- Go for a walk
- Brush your teeth with your opposite hand
- Switch from coffee to tea
- Cross your arms with the other one on top

Other ways in which you can mix things up...

_____

_____

_____

_____

_____

Start off with easy change. Then challenge yourself by introducing greater degrees of change in your life. Before long, you'll start to notice a difference in the way you think. You'll begin looking for new and different approaches to everyday problems; and creativity will flourish.

Let's tie this to your personal situation. On the next page, outline a typical day in your life. Don't be too general – it's better to include plenty of detail. Start with your morning routine, then move on to your routine at work. Then finish with typical activities once you get back home.

Give it a shot.

A day in your life (list your typical routine)

_____

_____

_____

_____

_____

_____

_____

_____

_____

_____

_____

_____

_____

_____

_____

Now... go back to the list you just created, and circle at least three things where you can start to introduce change. Get creative. Try to think of new and different ways to accomplish those items.

Try it now.

Great. Now for the hard part... It's really easy to sit there and say, "Yeah, that's a good idea. I should try that." without actually following through and implementing change. So commit to doing it; right now. At the very least, you'll stave off some of the boredom of your daily routine. If you're really committed to it, it could help start a wave of creativity that will open new doors and exciting opportunities in your life. What have you got to lose? So give it a shot.

3. Take advantage of your "me" time

For many of us, there are very few times in the day when we can stop and take a few minutes to be with our own thoughts. And if you have kids, you're probably saying, "yeah, right – forget it!"

But no matter who you are or what your life is like, there is one time available to you when you have complete control over what you think about. The trick is using the time wisely. I'm talking about that time when you first lie down to go to sleep. I like to call this period the "all-me time." This is that time when you know you won't have anyone interrupting you (in most cases, at least) or pulling you away from your train of thought. This is the one time of the day when you can think about anything you want. Think about that! You have absolute control. (And let's face it -- there aren't a lot of times when that is the case.) So take advantage of it!

Again… it's all in how you use this time. Here's what most of us tend to do: we lie there, worrying about what happened that day, what's going to happen the next day, why we didn't do this, when we're going to do that... etc., etc. But all that worrying does you absolutely no good. Remember -- be W.I.S.E. (If you don't remember what that stands for, go to page 30 and read that passage again.)

Here are some tips to help you get it right:

Do Not

- Worry about what happened that day.
- Worry about what's going to happen tomorrow.
- Make lists of what you need to do. This leads to the above.
- Re-enact bad moments in your head. You can't change it now.

Do

- Take yourself to a place that is relaxing and joyful.
- Think about all the great things in your life (this is an example of when your lists really come into play).
- Let loose. For example, if you always wanted to fly a plane but never had the chance, here's your opportunity. Again – you can think about *anything* you want. You can make anything possible during this time. Enjoy that freedom.

4. Be goofy

Most of us have a tendency to be a little too serious all the time. We spend so much time worrying about everything going on in our lives that we forget to take a moment or two to have a little fun.

So here's what I want you to do right now -- put this book down (remember that you're on page 55), and try to make a facial expression you've never made before. You'll have to get creative, and it may take a few tries. But challenge yourself to create a brand new facial expression (the weirder, the better).

Nice job. Now didn't that feel good? For those of you who were in a public place when you did this – double points for you. And if you noticed other people looking at you strangely while you were doing this – you get triple bonus points.

The point is, it's okay to be a little goofy. That's what makes this world so interesting. If everyone were serious all the time, we'd all be extremely bored with ourselves.

Stuffy is just that – stuffy. While you may think it's extremely important to be "professional" and serious, having some fun every now and then can do wonders for yourself and your career. After all, we like to be around those who make us feel good about ourselves. And having fun does exactly that.

I'm not saying you should go to business meetings with a fake arrow through the head. But being a constant stick-in-the-mud can do a lot more damage.

Let's go back to some important moments in your life. In the spaces on the following page, write down the top five goofiest moments in your life. These are times when you threw all inhibitions out the window and just had fun.

Top five goofiest moments of your life:

_____

_____

_____

_____

_____

Quick check… are you smiling right now? I'm willing to bet that you are. Because thinking back to those times when we were goofy in our lives evokes that emotion – it makes us happy.

Just because you're an adult now doesn't mean you can't have fun anymore. Let your hair down and allow yourself to be goofy. Because laughter really is the best medicine.

5. Get Outside

Look back to the daily routine you created for yourself on page 52. Now think about how much of your day is spent indoors. For most of us, we get up, prepare for work, go into the garage, get in our car, drive to work, spend all day inside, walk back to our car, drive home and sit in the house the rest of the evening.

Think about when you were a kid. Some of the best times you ever had were outside. Building a treehouse, riding your bike, playing ball, the list goes on and on. Somehow between childhood and adulthood, we decided to spend as little time outside as possible. It's time to fix that.

Next chance you get (preferably right now, if possible), go for a walk outside. I don't care if it's the middle of winter. Put on a coat and go for a walk. Take a look around and discover all the amazing things that are right in front of you. Then make that a regular part of your week. You'll be amazed at how good this can make you feel.

6. Stop procrastinating

This can be one of the most difficult things to overcome. With so much going on in our lives, it becomes very easy to say, "I'll start on it later..." Whether it's going for a walk outside, creating a plan for that new idea at work, or even something as simple as trying a new dessert, it's all too easy to put it off. One of the best ways to beat the tendency to procrastinate is to create a list of those things you need to do, and simply do them. You'll soon find that the great thing about tackling something that you've been putting off is the sense of accomplishment once that task is complete.

So let's get you started... in the spaces on the following page, write down all the things you've been putting off doing. Start small (buying a birthday gift, calling an old friend, etc.) and work your way up to the big ones (starting that remodeling project, taking a martial arts class, etc.). These are all the things you promised yourself long ago you would do, but just haven't found the time yet. Let's begin.

All the things you've been putting off:

_____

_____

_____

_____

_____

_____

_____

_____

Now take a moment to look over the list you just created and put a star next to <u>one thing</u> you're going to do <u>this week</u>. So within seven days, you're going to tackle at least one item on this list.

Once you start completing the tasks on your list, these successes will start to build on themselves, and you'll find yourself procrastinating less. Not only will you get more things done, but you'll also feel better about yourself in the process.

7. Do something that scares you

There are a lot of things out there that scare us. It can be something as monumental as changing careers; it can be something as simple as not drinking coffee in the morning. But there's certainly no shortage of things that make us feel uneasy.

It's time you started using this to your advantage. Taking on something that scares you, be it small or hugely significant, allows you to rise above and conquer that challenge. When you're successful at overcoming these challenges, it not only provides one more thing to add to your big list of accomplishments, but it also provides you with added self-confidence; and that's a winning combination. So the next time something is a little scary to you, don't back down.

Here's a personal example to show how important this can be... I enjoy riding motorcycles, both on and off road. A few years back, I was approached by another rider to join him on a trip to Mexico and back. The majority of my riding up to that point included day-trips around Arizona. This would be the first extended motorcycle trip of my life – and to a different country, no less. Needless to say, the idea was a little scary. Depending on who you ask, riding a motorcycle to Mexico can be extremely dangerous. I heard stories of crooked Federales, rampant banditos and even El Chupacabra (an elusive beast that sucks the blood of goats). Despite those stories, which you have to take with a grain of salt, there were more legitimate concerns, like US insurance companies not providing coverage south of the border. What if something happened down there – to the bike or to me?

I remember going back and forth as to whether or not I would make the trip. Even the night before leaving, I was contemplating the decision. But I overcame that fear, made the trip and had one of the best times of my entire life. (When I made my own list of personal accomplishments, that trip definitely made the list.)

A real eye opener for me on that trip was realizing that most people who warn you about heading out on adventures like this have no clue what they're talking about. There were no killer banditos, the Federales we did encounter (at various checkpoints in Mexico) were very professional and helpful, and there were certainly no blood-sucking monsters. In fact, I never once felt unsafe while there. Consequently, I've made many return trips to Mexico on a motorcycle, and have amazing memories to last a lifetime as a result.

The point is, you can't let fear stop you from experiencing new adventures. Challenge yourself to rise above and try something that is a little frightening. It doesn't have to be dangerous – it can be something as simple as getting a dog or taking a dance class.

It's time for another list. This time, capture the top five things that you've thought of doing, but the fear of tackling that challenge prevented you from actually trying. It may be something in the past, it may be something you're thinking about doing.

There may be some overlap with previous lists you created. That's okay. Fear is one of the most common reasons we put something off until "later." But for this list, try to include those items that really challenge you to rise above your fear.

Top five things you wanted to do, but fear got in the way

_____

_____

_____

_____

_____

Chapter five:
The Importance of Dreams

"We grow great by dreams ... Some of us let these great dreams die, but others nourish and protect them; nurse them through bad days till they flourish; bring them to the sunshine and light..."
- Woodrow Wilson

Let's talk about your dreams for a few moments. No, not the ones that come to you when you're sleeping, but the hopes, dreams and aspirations that carry us into every new day.

Dreams can be monumental aspirations or they can be seemingly minor goals. But they all share one thing in common -- they give you hope for what comes next. They provide us something to look forward to, and encourage us to do better in our everyday lives.

Throughout history, there are countless examples of how one person's dream turned into an idea that changed the world. Stop for a moment and look around where you're sitting right now. Everything you see, be it an airplane, a chair or even something as small as a salt shaker, all started off as someone's dream.

Let's think for a minute about some of the dreams that have most impacted the world as we know it...

- Electricity
- The light bulb
- Antibiotics
- The internal combustion engine
- The Internet
- Radio and TV broadcasting
- The printing press

Every one of these dreams started with a person or a team of people who decided it was time to make something happen. And the result was something incredible.

But it's easy to look at ideas like these and say, "Yeah, but I'm no Thomas Edison. There's no way I could come up with an idea that significant. Those people are on a different level."

Okay, how about some of the dreams that weren't quite so significant, but nonetheless led to new ideas that made this world a better place? Here are a few examples of what I'm talking about:

- Safety pins
- Tissue paper
- Scotch tape
- Coffee stirrers
- The toothbrush
- Batteries
- The ballpoint pen
- Breath mints
- Staplers
- Zippers

This list could go on for another 200 pages. The point is, every one of these items were dreamt up by "normal" people like yourself. The majority of them weren't geniuses. They just refused to give up on their ideas.

Dreaming doesn't have to mean creating something altogether new. It can simply be planning for what you want to do tomorrow, next week or even five years from now. You can also have dreams for other people like your family and friends. The thing to keep in mind when thinking through goals and aspirations for other people is that you have much less control over what they do. You can guide and influence them, but what they do is ultimately up to them. So don't beat yourself up too much (or think less of them) if the dreams for others don't become reality.

But let's start with you. In the spaces on the following page, write down the goals, aspirations and dreams for yourself. Think through want you want to do next week, next month and next year to help yourself grow and learn. This is an important list, so take some time and give it some real thought. (Answers like "make my children happy" don't count. It's a nice gesture, but they'll do fine on their own. This list is for your personal development – not those around you.)

Your dreams, goals and aspirations

_____

_____

_____

_____

_____

_____

_____

_____

When you were a kid, you had dreams of what you were going to do when you grew up. For a lot of us, what we're doing now in no way resembles those early dreams. (I was certain I was going to be an astronaut.) But that's okay. It certainly doesn't mean we're failures.

Here's the great thing about dreams – as we get older, we become better able to make our dreams a reality. The most important aspect of this is the fact that we get better at fine-tuning our goals and aspirations. While I still think it would be pretty amazing to be an astronaut, I now know that it's not a feasible goal for me. So I can still imagine myself flying through the stars, but I have no expectation of that coming true. Instead, I can start making plans that are more suited to the way my life has developed, and create new dreams for myself.

So don't get bogged down in thinking that you're a failure if the dreams you had when you were 14 (or 24, for that matter) haven't come true. That's what leads to most mid-life crises... and no, a Porsche won't solve your problems.

Let's do a little comparison. In the spaces below, write down the dreams, goals and aspirations you had when you were younger. They could be career related; they could be about material possessions; they could be about your family life. These are the things you wanted to do "when you grew up."

_____

_____

_____

_____

_____

_____

_____

_____

Now compare the list on the previous page with the one you created on page 67. Are there any items that are similar on both lists? If not, that's perfectly all right. (There really are no wrong answers here.) But chances are, there are quite a few differences between the two lists. That's simply a natural part of growing and developing.

For those of you with children -- don't forget that you still need to regularly think through goals and aspirations for yourself. All too often, we focus so much on the dreams we have for our kids, that we forget to spend time on what it is we want out of life. Between flag-football, band practice and parent-teacher meetings, we don't think we have time to stop and make plans for our continuing development. One thing's for certain... if you keep telling yourself you don't have time, you never will.

So how are you supposed to do it, then? When you're juggling schedules for four kids, how do you make time for yourself?

First off, try not to constantly worry about the fate of your children. I know... easier said than done. But you can spend countless hours thinking through how their lives are going to develop. No matter how good those plans are, chances are your kids are going to do something to get in the way of those plans. It's called growing up; and you don't have as much control over it as you would like. Give them some healthy goals and aspirations, and do as much as you can to provide them the means to pursue those goals. Most of all, don't be surprised when the goals they pursue don't even remotely resemble what you had planned for them.

Now that you're spending a little less time worrying about your kids, start setting aside time to think through continuing goals for yourself, and what it will take to accomplish those goals. It may be you'll only have fifteen minutes in the day to do this. *But find those fifteen minutes and guard them with your life.*

Back to your dreams... take a look at the list you created on page 67 (your current list of goals and aspirations). I want you to choose <u>one</u> of those. You're going to focus on that one dream and think through what it's going to take to make that a reality. So pick one you want to make happen sooner than later and write it in the space below.

_____

Whether you chose a lofty goal like learning a new language or one that is simple to implement, you're going to need a game plan. So take the next few minutes to think through everything that will have to happen for you to achieve this goal. List every step that will be necessary.

Steps to achieve your goal

_____

_____

_____

_____

_____

_____

_____

Once you've outlined the steps needed to make this goal achievable, it's simply a matter of organizing those steps and actually doing them.

Now give yourself a due date for each step. To the right of each one, write in the date by which you want to have that step completed. Then stick to those dates. Don't let yourself slip. Make it happen.

Once you've achieved that goal, start all over with another one. The most difficult part in all of this is simply convincing yourself that you're going to do it.

No matter how busy you get; no matter how many other things are happening in your life; you are going to make this one thing happen.

Chapter six:
Playing to Your Strengths
(and Weaknesses)

"Enter every activity without giving mental recognition to the possibility of defeat. Concentrate on your strengths, instead of your weaknesses... on your powers, instead of your problems"
- Paul J. Meyer

We all have strengths and weaknesses; and the combination of the two is going to be unique for every single person on this planet. That's pretty amazing if you really stop to think about it... out of several billion people who are living right now, not one of them shares the same set of strengths and weaknesses as you.

So what are yours? Let's take a quick evaluation. In the spaces below, write down your strengths. By strengths, we mean skills, knowledge and anything you're gifted at. This can be much more difficult than you might initially think. Some of us find it hard to think about the things that we do well. But dig deep – and don't hold back.

Your Strengths

_____

_____

_____

_____

_____

_____

_____

Good. Now let's do the same for your weaknesses.

Your Weaknesses

_____

_____

_____

_____

_____

_____

_____

_____

Now that you've listed your strengths and weaknesses, what's next? How do we put that info to practical use?

Let's start off by separating out strengths and weaknesses that are **A) internal**, or only known by you and **B) external**, or those that are visible by others. For example, if one of the strengths you listed was the ability to remember details and figures, is that trait readily noticeable by those who work around you? If it isn't, then put an **"I"** to the left of the item on the list. If the trait is known by others, put an **"E"** to the left of the item.

Go ahead and take a couple of minutes to do this for each of the strengths and weaknesses you listed.

Now take a look at your modified list (with items marked as internal or external). For those strengths that you marked as internal, think about how you can make those strengths more visible to those around you – especially your boss. (Think back to the exercise we discussed on page 19 about discussing your accomplishments with those around you.) Conversely, look at the weaknesses that you marked as external. For those items, think about how you can make a better effort to reduce the visibility of those items to others around you. For example, if you listed "losing my temper" as an external weakness, work on ways that you can vent your frustrations in a more private setting, so that others don't see this trait as often.

Here are some additional suggestions on how to utilize your lists of strengths and weaknesses:

Use your strengths
You probably think you're already doing a decent job of utilizing your strengths. After all, they are the things that you're best at, right? But in reality, most people greatly underutilize their personal strengths. You need to make a conscious effort to keep your strengths in mind in your daily activities, so that you'll be able to utilize them to a greater degree.

Develop your strengths
Just because you're already good at something doesn't mean you can't get better. Your existing strengths are what have allowed you to do some amazing things. If you continue to develop those strengths, it will help you reach new levels of success. (Plus, in the process of developing your current strengths, you might even develop some new ones.)

Look for new ways to use those strengths

In addition to further developing your strengths, explore how you can use them in new and different ways. For example, if one of the strengths you listed was "works well in a team setting," look for ways that you can get more involved with teams of other employees. Start a committee that comes up with ideas on how to further improve service to your customers. Or one that looks for fun activities that allow employees to socialize after work.

Don't ignore your weaknesses

Some people think that you should simply forget about your weaknesses. The reasoning usually being, "why focus on the negative?" But forgetting about your weaknesses doesn't help you improve upon them (or even mask them). Everybody has their own set of weaknesses, but many of those items can be improved upon, and some even eliminated. Start by highlighting those items that you feel you can work on.

Work on those where improvement is possible

Once you've identified the weaknesses that do allow room for improvement, take active measures to try and minimize or eliminate those weaknesses. If there are external forces that perpetuate these items, think about what it would take to separate yourself from those external influences. Create an action plan and stick to it. Force yourself to really work on improving.

There will be some weaknesses that you won't be able to overcome. (This is natural.) However, you can make some of these weaknesses less visible to others – thereby turning external items into internal weaknesses.

Don't forget that weaknesses can be turned into strengths in certain cases. Think about each item and determine if it's possible with a little work to turn that weakness around.

Get help

Whether you're looking to develop your strengths or minimize your weaknesses, help is available. One of the best ways to make progress is discussing these items with a close personal friend or family member. They're likely to be very honest with you in measuring the true nature of each item, and can help you in coming up with ideas on how to improve.

Focus more on your strengths than your weaknesses

Human nature often makes us think more about what's wrong with us than what's right. But fight the urge to focus on the negative and spend twice as much time thinking through all of your strengths. By playing to and developing your strengths, you'll be automatically negating some of the weaknesses at the same time. And by concentrating more on what you're really good at, you'll also benefit from increased self confidence and better self esteem.

Chapter Seven:
Is It Time You Fired Your Job?

*Most people spend more time at work
than they do with their families.
Make that time count.*

This chapter is intended to help you evaluate your current job. Because work is such a large part of our lives, it's important that we be happy in our jobs. If we're not, we need to look at making a change. So whether you've considered looking for a new (or better) career, you're unhappy in you current job but are reluctant to make a change, or if you're simply curious whether there's something better out there, the information in this chapter can help.

If you currently enjoy what you do for a living (and there are a lot of people who do), then go ahead and skip ahead to page 91.

Match your career to your skills.

Unless you're independently wealthy, you're going to have to work for a living (like the rest of us). It's just a fact of life. In fact, most adults spend more than 60% of their waking hours at work. So if you're going to spend more than half of your adult life on the job, you might as well enjoy it. It's one of the oldest clichés around, but it also happens to be true: life is short.

If you're not enjoying what you're doing, you need to make a change.

When it comes to change, making a bold decision regarding one's job is one of the most difficult things to face. After all, this is our livelihood we're talking about. "Without my job, I can't pay the bills." In most cases, however, this is simply an excuse that helps us deal with not taking that risk.

Everyone I've known who made a significant change regarding their career has ended up in a better place than where they started (whether that decision was theirs or was forced on them).

That doesn't mean you should quit your job tomorrow. It simply means you should consider all of your options – especially those that are better suited to your skill set. It could be a different position at your current company, it could mean changing careers altogether. But you need to be honest with yourself and determine whether or not a change is needed.

It's time to create a couple of additional lists. These will help you to sit down and objectively consider where you're at currently, and where you need to be.

In the spaces below, write down the **things you like most about your current job**. These are the things that make you feel good about going in to work every day.

_____

_____

_____

_____

_____

_____

_____

Great. Now use the spaces below to write down the **things you like least about your current job**. These are the things that cause you the most tension and frustration.

_____

_____

_____

_____

_____

_____

_____

Now compare the two lists you just created. Do the items on the list of things that frustrate you outweigh the positives, or vice versa?

Now go back to each list and put an asterisk next to those items that are exclusive to your current employer. For example, if you listed "my boss doesn't give me any respect," that would be exclusive to your present company, because that boss won't be found at another company. (That's not to say a supervisor at another company couldn't act in a similar fashion, but at least it won't be the same person.) Go ahead and mark those items.

Think about those items you just highlighted. These are the positive things that are tying you to your current job as well as those that might convince you to look for a change.

Now, assuming the items on the frustrations list are fairly significant, it's time to tackle one of the hardest things you're likely to encounter... convincing yourself to commit to making a change. This is a big, scary decision that scares off a lot of people. It's very easy to say to yourself, "You know, it's not really that bad. I probably won't find anything better than this." And you give up.

Changing anything about your life is a difficult thing to do. But changing jobs has to rank up there as one of the most daunting things you'll encounter. But you can't shy away from it. Your happiness and that of your family is simply too important. This doesn't mean you have to walk in and give your notice tomorrow. But you can start the process of seeing what else is out there.

In today's world, finding a better job has gotten a lot easier. First off, the resources available to help you with your search have grown exponentially over the past decade. Consider this... as little as ten years ago, the most prevalent way to learn about job openings was checking the classifieds in the local paper. If you wanted to look for jobs in other cities, that also meant picking up a local paper from each of those regions. Today, you can search literally hundreds of online job classified databases from your home computer. Sites like Monster.com and Hotjobs.com have some of the most robust listings of available jobs. Another great place to look is on company web sites. A lot of companies include available job listings on their private sites. It's a safe bet that in one afternoon, you would be able to find quite a number of postings that attract your attention.

Another example of how the marketplace has changed is more prevalent use of flextime and telecommuting. I know a lot of people who have great jobs (and earn a decent living) working right out of their homes. So just because a great employer is four hours away doesn't necessarily mean that you won't be able to work for them.

What if you're thinking about changing careers altogether, but want more information on what it's really like to work over at company X? One thing you might consider is setting up informational interviews with people who already work for that company. This is a great way to not only learn more about a different employer, but also introduce yourself and create a good first impression. So if a job opening does come up within that organization, you'll be the first person they call. Here's how it works...

Step 1 - Identify organizations you'd like to interview

It's time to do some research. Set aside an hour or two where you can sit at a computer and devote some time to finding some potentially great places to work. Don't limit yourself... the majority of your experience may have come from working in a particular industry. But the skills and qualifications you've developed could easily be applied in other industries. (In many cases, it may even be a better fit for unlocking your potential.)

While doing your research, don't limit yourself by only checking job postings. There may be a perfect job out there with your name written all over it; but it simply hasn't been posted yet. Instead, look for information on companies that interest you. Ones where you think the corporate culture and opportunities would be a great fit for what you're looking for. Even if those companies don't have openings right now, you still want to learn more about them.

Step 2 - Get yourself in front of the decision maker

Once you've identified a few companies that really pique your interest, find out who the decision maker is in the department that interests you. Check the company web site for contact information or press releases.

If that doesn't work, call up the main number and ask for someone in that department.

Once you've found out the name of the appropriate person, write him/her a letter asking to set up a brief meeting so you can learn more about their company. Here's an example of what that might look like:

"I'm writing you because I'm considering a career change, and I'm looking for more information on how different companies approach (functional area) within (industry). I'm not looking for a job; I'd simply like to draw from your knowledge and experience to learn more about this area. This would only take about 15-20 minutes of your time. I greatly appreciate your assistance and will call you in a few days to see which date works best for you."

Setting up a meeting like this won't be easy. In many cases, you'll hit that infamous roadblock known as the receptionist. But don't give up. Get creative and try different approaches to get yourself in front of the right person.

Step 3 - Conduct an informational interview

Once you've succeeded in setting up a meeting, write down some questions that will help you get a better feel for what it's like to work at this company (and in that department). Remember, the goal is to determine whether or not it's worth it for you to make a change. But more importantly, this type of a meeting allows you the opportunity to share your strengths with a potential employer.

This is important: you don't want to ever give the impression that you're "fishing" for a job. If the person you're meeting with thinks this, the meeting will be cut short, and you'll have wasted a perfect opportunity to make a great impression. Instead, reiterate that you're not looking for job; you're simply looking to learn more about that company/position/industry.

That doesn't mean you can't share your resume with the individual. If you present it in the right way, you'll be able to share your skills and qualifications without making the decision maker feel like you're looking for a job.

Start off by asking their opinions about the industry. What do/don't they like about it? What are current trends that are affecting the industry? Make them feel at ease by talking about themselves.

Then switch the point of focus by asking about the most important skills and qualifications needed for someone to be successful in that department. Once they've shared that information, you can then pull out your information and ask if your background would be a good fit for a company that was hiring for that role.

At the very least, you'll learn more about what it's like to work for that company. But the most important benefit of conducting these meetings is planting a seed that if an opportunity becomes available at that organization, you're a great candidate to contact.

So if you're not happy in your current job, don't be afraid to start looking. It's a really big world out there, and if you devote some time to it, you're bound to find something that's a great fit.

Chapter Eight:
If You Only Remember One Thing...

"You have it easily in your power to increase the sum total of this world's happiness now. How? By giving a few words of sincere appreciation to someone who is lonely or discouraged. Perhaps you will forget tomorrow the kind words you say today, but the recipient may cherish them over a lifetime."
- Dale Carnegie

If you remember only one thing after reading this book, it should be the following...

Always appreciate what's around you – the people, the things, the beauty, the flaws. This is the surest path to true happiness.

I can't over-emphasize the importance of appreciation; and yet it's so easy to forget about it. We get so involved in worrying about our lives that we fail to stop and appreciate all that we have.

And there's so much to appreciate! The things we've accomplished, the opportunities that lay ahead, the people in our lives, the comforts and conveniences, the companionship of a pet, or just the fact that we're here. In other words, life.

Time for another list. (And this is one of those important ones...) On the following pages, write down anything and everything that you appreciate in your life. Don't forget to include the following:

- **People** (your friends, family, co-workers or even the great cashier at the local coffee shop)

- **Things** (your prized possessions, that favorite shirt, your car)

- **Yourself** (what you've been able to do, what lies ahead for you, your strengths, your abilities, your health)

- **All the other stuff** (all those unsung little things that make life worth living)

Nothing is too big or too small for this list. Try to get as much as you can down on paper.

Everything You Appreciate

Everything You Appreciate, continued

_____

_____

_____

_____

_____

_____

_____

_____

_____

_____

_____

_____

_____

_____

_____

Hopefully, you ran out of space because you realized there are so many things to be thankful for in your life. If you didn't use both pages, I challenge you to go back and try again. Think about the little things that bring a smile to your face. It could be something as seemingly unimportant as that down comforter on your bed or as grand as the sound of your child's laughter. But get as much as you can on those two pages.

Great. Now I'd like you to think through the following: go back over the list you just created and put an asterisk next to every line item that you've taken for granted. (If you're like me when I did this, you're going to see a lot of asterisks...)

The problem is, we rarely take the time to stop and really think about all the things that make our lives so great.

So turn that around right now...

Chapter Nine:
Be a Hero

"Everyone is necessarily the hero of his own life story."
- John Barth

We all need heroes in our lives. When we're young, it's easy to find a hero in our favorite comic book, sports team or movie character. We look at these larger-than-life individuals and think, "wouldn't it be great to live like that?"

But as we become adults, we spend less and less time thinking about our heroes. After all, we can't exactly fly like Superman (or even Michael Jordan, for that matter). So we begin to forget about what it means to have heroes in our lives.

But what we often fail to recognize is that heroism is all around us. The great thing about being a hero is that there are no predetermining qualifications. Anyone can be a hero – whether it's a great teacher, a friendly and helpful employee, a loving mother or even a homeless person. Because being a hero has nothing to do with who you are or what you have; it's all about *what you do.*

Believe it or not, you have been a hero to someone else at some point in your life. And chances are, you could be looked upon as a hero right now. Being a hero doesn't mean you have to do some incredibly courageous act like rescue an old lady from a purse snatcher. Even the smallest thing could make you a hero through the eyes of another person.

Another way of thinking about heroism is focusing on those people that have provided you with inspiration. So let's take a couple of minutes to recognize those who have been an inspiration to you. Think about those people who have been a hero to you at some point or another and write the names in the spaces on the following page.

Those who have been a hero to you

_____	_____
_____	_____
_____	_____
_____	_____
_____	_____
_____	_____
_____	_____
_____	_____

Think about the people on this list. What was it they did that made you think so highly of them? You may be surprised to find that it wasn't some monumental feat. In many cases, our heroes are those individuals who simply took the time to do the right thing. That's all it takes.

Here's an example from personal experience of someone who performed a reasonably simple task that made me think, "Wow, I really respect that."

A few months back, I was driving home from work when I saw a car stopped in the road ahead with its hazard lights on. As I pulled up behind the car, I saw a man out in front picking up some debris that had been left in the road by another vehicle. When I called out to see if everything was all right, he stated, "Yeah, I just didn't want someone to hit this stuff and damage their car." Then he waived, got back in his car and took off.

As I started driving again, I remember thinking how nice it was of that guy to stop and clean the road so others wouldn't hit the debris. While most people would have simply driven around the debris, he was considerate enough to remove the hazard. That was a heroic thing to do. If I ever see that man again, I'll shake his hand and say thanks.

The thing to remember about all of this is that anyone can be a hero – especially you. And whether you realize it or not, you've been a hero to several people throughout the course of your life.

You can be a hero to anyone around you. Your coworkers, your boss, your kids (at least, until they reach the teenage years), your friends, the guy working behind the counter at the video store or even a stranger you pass by on the street. You can also be a hero to yourself.

Here's something to remember about heroes – they don't do it for the recognition. They do it because *it's the right thing to do.* So don't let it bother you if you do something really nice for someone, and it doesn't seem to be appreciated. Even if you're not a hero to that person, you will be to yourself.

It's time to recognize the hero in you. In the spaces on the following page, write down a few times when you did the right thing (which made you a hero at the time). Remember, it doesn't have to be a monumentally amazing thing. Even the simplest action can be heroic.

Times in your life when you did the right thing

You see? There were (and will be) times when you really were a hero.
It's about time you started recognizing yourself as one. **So we're
going to have you choose a name and create a costume for the hero
you play every day.**

Let's start off with your hero name. Take a few minutes to play
around with some ideas in your head. Here are some adjectives to help
you think of what you might want to include in your hero name...

*Amazing • Cool Headed • Considerate • Hilarious • Caring • Superb •
Friendly • Happy • Awesome • Intriguing • Adventurous • Stupendous •
Brilliant • Outstanding • Exceptional • Admirable • Tremendous •
Marvelous • Wonderful • Remarkable • Terrific • Magnificent •
Sensational • Splendid • Radiant • Noble • Decent • Gallant •
Courteous • Thoughtful • Kind • Selfless • Helpful*

OK... let's hear it. Write your hero name in the space below.

_____

Great! Now create a logo for your hero name. Try to think of a symbol or letters that encapsulate the name you chose and draw it inside the shape below.

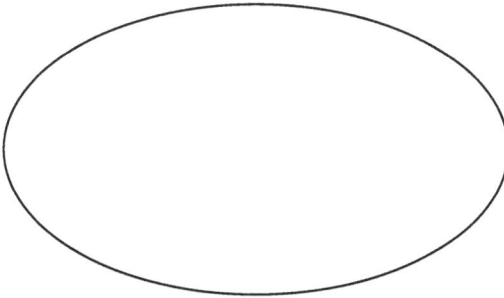

Now let's put it all together. On the blank figure on the following page, draw out your hero costume. Don't forget to include your new logo on the chest of your costume as well as your hero name underneath. Here are some things you might want to include on your costume:

- A jacket or cape
- Color
- Gloves

- A utility belt
- Boots
- A helmet or mask

Have fun with it!

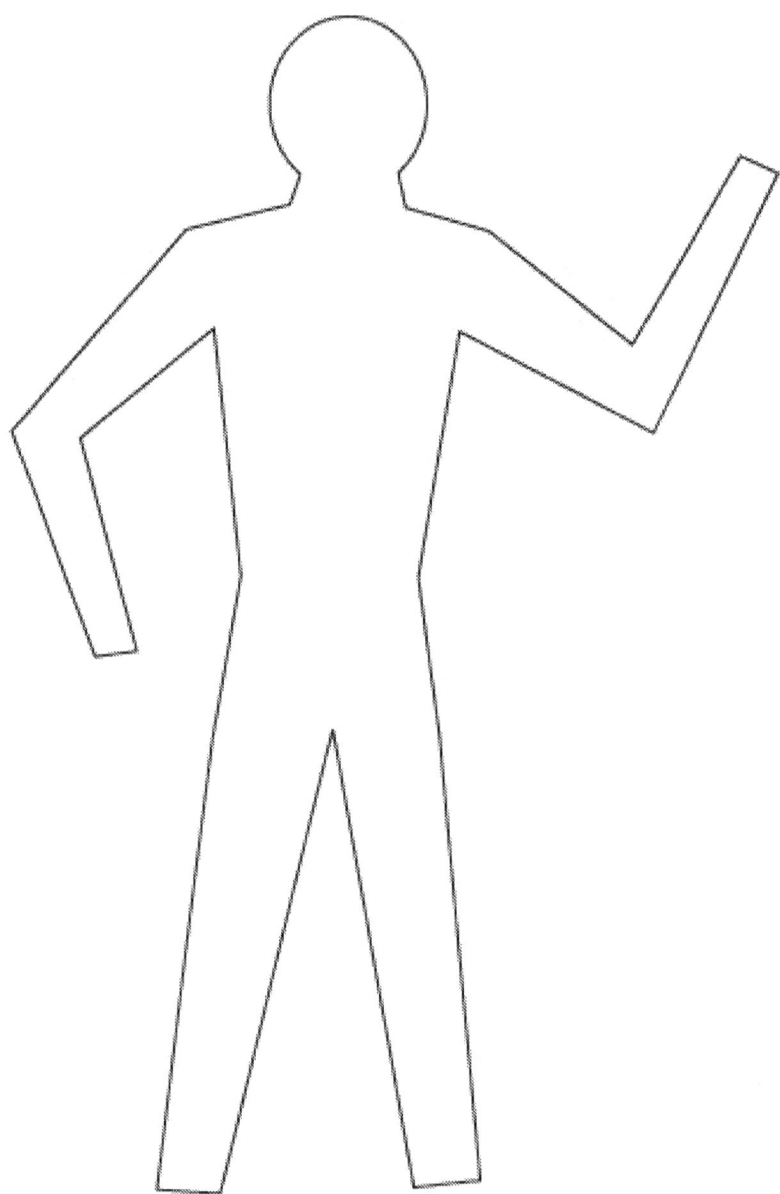

Now that we've identified that you're a legitimate hero (including an official logo and costume), let's talk about what you can do to maintain your hero status. Here are a couple of simple rules to follow as a hero:

Hero rule #1 - Fight the Forces of Evil

While most of us won't ever have to go head-to-head with a master villain bent on world domination, we do face the forces of negativity every single day. And negativity can be a pretty evil thing. So do your best to fight off negativity both for yourself and for those around you. You've already been equipped with a super-power to help you with this – your smile. If you see someone being confronted with negativity, stop and give them a nice, genuine smile. You'll be amazed at the power of this.

Hero rule #2 - Always Do the Right Thing

Every once in a while, you'll be presented with an opportunity to either do the right thing or take the easy way out. It might be something as simple as stopping for 60 seconds to safely move some debris off the road. It may be helping out a co-worker on a project *before* they ask for assistance. Or it could be something as important as giving blood. But in nearly every situation, you'll know the right thing to do. You just need to make the decision to do it.

Be that hero.

Chapter Ten:
Putting It All Together

"Whatever you can do or dream you can, begin it.
Boldness has genius, power, and magic in it. Begin it now."
- Goethe

We've covered a lot throughout this book. To help put it all together, we're going to have you create an action plan. To do this, you'll first need to capture some of the highlights of what was covered thus far. So we'll start by having you fill in the following sections.

Your greatest accomplishments

Take a look at the list of your greatest accomplishments (on pages 9-10) as well as your list of professional accomplishments (on page 15). From those two lists, highlight the top ten things that you're most proud of; then write those ten items in the space below.

_____

_____

_____

_____

_____

_____

_____

_____

_____

_____

This list can give you strength, confidence and the ability to instantly bring a smile to your face. These are some amazing things that you should make you swell with pride. Think about the items on this list whenever you need encouragement or even a quick pick-me-up.

Grab some index card or Post-It notes, and tape these up where you'll need them most (at the office, on your personal computer, etc.). You'll be amazed how effective these reminders can be at helping you tackle new ideas and projects. Before long, you'll be adding brand new items to this list!

Your unique skill set

Take a look at the list on page 16. These are the skills and abilities that have helped you accomplish some truly great things. These are also what will allow you to continue to excel. In the spaces below, write down your top five skills and abilities:

_____

_____

_____

_____

_____

Great! Now write on the following page at least five skills and abilities that you would like to develop or enhance. (These could come from your existing list of skills, or could be ones that you want to add to your list.) Put another way, these are things you want to learn to do better.

Skills and/or abilities you would like to further develop:

_____

_____

_____

_____

_____

You've now identified areas where you'd like to improve as an individual. So let's think through how you're going to accomplish this. In the spaces below, write down the steps you need to take develop the skills you just listed. There's also space for you to include start dates. Think about those dates realistically, and stick to them!

How and when you're going to further develop your skill set:

Start Date

_____   _____

_____   _____

_____   _____

_____   _____

_____   _____

Don't forget to share your list of skills and accomplishments with your boss. This is an important step to helping your company see the value that you can provide. See pages 19-20 for information how to set up that meeting.

Ways you can mix it up

On page 50, you listed some ways in which you could introduce change in your life by doing a few things a little differently. Then, on page 52, you circled things out of your daily routine that you're going to try differently. It's important that you follow through and actually apply that change, so let's re-list what those items are. In the spaces below, write those things out of your daily routine that you're going to change up. (These should be the items that you previously circled on your list on page 52.)

_____

_____

_____

_____

_____

Doing those things you've always wanted to do

On page 61, you created a list of the top things you always wanted to do, but didn't (because you didn't think you could). Here's your chance to fix that. Pick one item from that list and write it in the space below. We'll then create an action plan on how you're going to begin the process of making this happen.

The number one thing you've always wanted to do (but haven't):

_____

Now that you've selected your one item, start thinking though the steps you'll need to take to actually make this happen. Don't get caught up in the "yeah, but..." mentality. As soon as you start saying things like "Yeah, but I don't have time to do that," you've already given up. You CAN do it. You just have to _allow_ yourself to do it. That starts with blocking out all those "yeah, but" thoughts.

So let's get started on your plan. In the spaces below, write out the sequential steps you'll need to take to help you accomplish that thing you've always wanted to do. Once again, you're going to list start dates for each step. It's very important that you hit these key dates to make sure you stay on course.

Start Date

_____   _____

_____   _____

_____   _____

_____   _____

_____   _____

Remember, don't let *that little voice* talk you out of accomplishing your dreams. You have the capabilities; you just need the self-confidence to make it happen.

Once you are successful in making this happen, pick another item on you list and start working toward that goal. That's the amazing thing about this process... the more you do it, the easier it becomes to start accomplishing those things that you previously thought were unattainable.

While the items listed in this review chapter are all important things for you to follow up on, don't forget to go back and review every chapter in this book. You took the time to process and record some valuable information that will help in your everyday life. Put that information to good use. It's easier than you think!

Chapter Eleven:
Resources To Help You

If you've wanted to do this...	Go here for info on how to get started*
Start a business	www.sba.gov/starting_business/
Go skydiving	www.dropzone.com
Drive a race car	www.racingschools.com/rs/
Write a book	www.jojaffa.com/guides/writeabook.htm
	www.writerswrite.com
Climb a mountain	www.aboutsports.org/s1/Climbing.php
	www.climbing.about.com
Start painting	www.watercolorpainting.com/watercolor-tutorials.htm
Start a home improvement project	www.doityourself.com
Go to an exotic foreign land	http://travel.state.gov
Ride a horse	www.learnhorseriding.com
Learn to sail	www.sailnet.com/forums/featured-articles/
Build a home theater	www.projectorpeople.com (resource zone)
For anything else you need to know	start with a search on Google.com

*The author has no affiliations with the above listed sites and does not guarantee the information contained therein will actually help you. But hey – sometimes all you need is a little info to get us headed in the right direction.

Additional spaces for notes, extra items on your lists, etc.

_____

_____

_____

_____

_____

_____

_____

_____

_____

_____

_____

_____

_____

_____

_____

Additional spaces for notes, extra items on your lists, etc

Additional spaces for notes, extra items on your lists, etc.

_____

_____

_____

_____

_____

_____

_____

_____

_____

_____

_____

_____

_____

_____

_____

Additional spaces for notes, extra items on your lists, etc.

_____

_____

_____

_____

_____

_____

_____

_____

_____

_____

_____

_____

_____

_____

_____

_____

_____

www.ingramcontent.com/pod-product-compliance
Lightning Source LLC
Chambersburg PA
CBHW031857090426
42741CB00005B/536